DATE DUE

APR 2 9 '09			
MAY 1 3 '09			
OCT 1 5 '09			
OCT 2 2 '09			
OCT 2 7 '09			
NOV 1 7 '09			
DEC 0 7 '09			
JAN 0 5 '09			
FEB 0 2 '10			
MAR 1 8 '10			
OCT 2 7 '10			
MAR 2 8 '11			
APR 1 1 '11			
APR 1 1 '11			

APR 1 4 '09

On the Front Lines

The U.S. Marine Corps at War

by Melissa Abramovitz

Consultant:
Thomas J. Evelyn
Lieutenant Colonel, Aviation
U.S. Army

CAPSTONE
HIGH-INTEREST
BOOKS

an imprint of Capstone Press
Mankato, Minnesota

Capstone High-Interest Books are published by Capstone Press
151 Good Counsel Drive, P.O. Box 669, Mankato, Minnesota 56002
http://www.capstone-press.com

Library of Congress Cataloging-in-Publication Data
Abramovitz, Melissa, 1954–
    The U.S. Marine Corps at war/by Melissa Abramovitz.
    p. cm.—(On the front lines)
    Includes bibliographical references and index.
    ISBN 0-7368-0923-6
    1. United States. Marine Corps—Juvenile literature. 2. United States.
Marine Corps—History—Juvenile literature. [1. United States. Marine Corps.]
I. Title. II. Series.
VE23 .A917 2002
359.9'6'0973—dc21   2001000448

Summary: Gives an overview of the U.S. Marine Corps, its mission, members,
history, recent conflicts, and modern equipment.

Editorial Credits
Blake Hoena, editor; Karen Risch, product planning editor; Steve Christensen,
    cover designer and illustrator; Katy Kudela, photo researcher

Photo Credits
Defense Visual Information Center, cover, 4, 7, 9, 14, 16, 19, 20, 22–23, 24, 27,
    28
North Wind Picture Archives, 10

2 3 4 5 6 07 06 05 04 03 02

Table of Contents

Features

CHAPTER 1

Learn about:

■ The Gulf War

■ Marine Corps mission

■ Marine Corps jobs

Marines use amphibious ships.

The U.S. Marine Corps

In 1990, Iraq invaded the Middle East country of Kuwait. The United States and its allies wanted to free Kuwait from Iraqi control. Allies are countries that work together. The U.S. and allied military leaders sent troops to the Middle East. These events led to the Gulf War (1991).

Before the fighting began, 17,000 U.S. Marines waited aboard amphibious ships in the Persian Gulf. These ships carry troops from the sea to the shore. The troops were preparing to attack Iraqi forces in Kuwait.

But the Marines did not attack. Iraqi forces had placed more than 1,000 mines in the Persian Gulf. These devices explode when ships come near or touch them. U.S. military leaders thought the attack would be too dangerous.

Instead, U.S. military leaders wanted to fool Iraqi leaders. They hoped Iraqi leaders would believe that the Marines were going to attack.

This plan worked. Iraqi military leaders sent 80,000 Iraqi troops to the Kuwaiti coast. The troops' mission was to defend Iraq against the Marines.

On February 24, 1991, the ground war began in the Gulf War. The United States and its allies sent troops into Kuwait and Iraq. The troops entered these countries from Saudi Arabia. After only four days, the U.S. and allied forces had defeated the Iraqi military.

The Marine Corps Mission

The Marine Corps protects the United States by air, land, and sea. The Marine Corps is the smallest branch of the U.S. military. But it has played an important role in many conflicts. Marines often are the first troops involved in major conflicts.

The Marine Corps organizes its fighting forces into three main divisions. These divisions are the Marine Forces Atlantic, the Marine Forces Pacific, and the Marine Forces Reserve.

Marine Corps members also help guard government buildings. Marines guard the White House in Washington, D.C. Marines guard U.S. embassies. These government buildings are in other countries.

Marines use aircraft to perform their duties.

Marine Corps Members

People volunteer to serve in the military. People join the Marines as officers or enlisted members. Officers direct enlisted members in their duties. Both men and women serve as officers and enlisted members.

Marines can serve on active duty or in the reserves. Active duty members work full time for the Marine Corps. More than 170,000 people are active members of the Marines.

Reserve members work part time. They train one weekend each month and serve two full weeks each year. More than 30,000 people are in the Marine Reserves. These people can be called to active duty in emergencies.

Marine Jobs

Marines perform many types of jobs. Some work in combat areas. They may be infantry soldiers. These Marines fight on foot. Other Marines drive tanks. Pilots use helicopters and airplanes to attack enemy targets. Pilots also use aircraft to carry troops and supplies where needed.

Some Marines work in law enforcement or as lawyers. Marine military police (MPs) arrest Marines who break laws. Marine lawyers

Marines in the reserves train one weekend each month.

represent in court Marines who have been accused of a crime.

Technical jobs also are important in the Marine Corps. Some Marines operate and repair communications equipment such as radios and telephones. Mechanics repair and maintain vehicles and weapons.

CHAPTER 2

Learn about:

- **The first Marines**

- **Marine traditions**

- **Early wars**

Early Marines served aboard Navy ships.

Marine Corps History

In the late 1700s, the Continental Congress governed the 13 American colonies. Its members created an army to fight the British. The Continental Army fought to gain the colonies' freedom from British rule. This began the Revolutionary War (1775–1783).

On November 10, 1775, the Continental Congress created the Continental Marines. About 230 men served in the Continental Marines. They helped keep order aboard U.S. Navy ships. Navy sailors sometimes misbehaved and fought against their officers.

Marines in the Revolutionary War

Marines also fought in sea battles. They fired guns called muskets at troops aboard enemy ships. Marines also threw explosive devices such as grenades at troops on British ships.

Marines climbed aboard enemy ships when a U.S. and a British ship collided in battle. Marines then fought hand-to-hand against British troops. They fought with swords and bayonets. Soldiers attached these metal blades to the end of their muskets.

The Continental Marines performed their first amphibious attack in 1776. They attacked British forces on New Providence Island in the Bahamas. They captured British cannons and gunpowder during this attack.

Marine Corps Traditions

Some of the Marine Corps traditions and symbols come from the Revolutionary War. The term "leatherneck" is still used as a nickname for Marines. This term comes from the leather collars that Continental Marines wore. They wore these neck pieces to protect themselves from sword injuries in battle.

Important Dates

1775—Revolutionary War begins; the Continental Congress creates the Continental Marines to keep order on Navy ships.

1776—Marines perform their first amphibious assault; they attack British forces on New Providence Island.

1798—U.S. government passes the Marine Corps Act.

1861—Civil War begins; Northern states fight against Southern states; the Northern states' victory helps end slavery.

1898—Spanish-American War begins.

1914—World War I begins; the United States enters the war in 1917.

1918—Opha Mae Johnson becomes the first woman to serve in the Marine Corps.

1939—World War II begins; the United States enters the war in 1941.

1950—Korean War begins.

1954—Vietnam War begins; the United States starts sending troops to Vietnam in the early 1960s.

1991—The Gulf War begins.

1992—Operation Restore Hope begins in Somalia.

Marines fought during World War II.

Continental Marines also wore a quatrefoil on their hats. This gold cord allowed Marine sharpshooters to recognize their own soldiers from enemy troops. Marines then would not accidentally shoot their own soldiers. Today, Marine officers wear a quatrefoil on their dress uniform.

After the Revolutionary War

The U.S. Congress disbanded the Continental Marines after the Revolutionary War. Congress members did not believe that the military needed Marines.

But in 1798, Congress realized that the Navy needed help protecting trading ships from pirate attacks. Congress then passed the Marine Corps Act on July 11, 1798. This law made the Marine Corps an official part of the U.S. military. The new Marine Corps had 25 officers and 58 enlisted members.

The Marine Mission

The Marines have fought in all major wars in which the United States has been involved. They performed many air, land, and sea missions during World War I (1914–1918). Marines helped capture Japanese-controlled islands in the Pacific Ocean during World War II (1939–1945). The Marines also performed amphibious assaults during the Korean War (1950–1953) and the Vietnam War (1954–1975).

CHAPTER 3

Learn about:

- **The Gulf War**

- **Marine Corps weapons**

- **Operation Restore Hope**

Marines used M-60 tanks during the Gulf War.

Recent Conflicts

The Marines have played an important role in many recent conflicts. They often are the first U.S. troops to respond to an emergency.

The Gulf War

In 1991, Marines fought in the Gulf War. The military called the attack on Iraqi forces in Kuwait "Operation Desert Storm."

Iraq invaded Kuwait on August 8, 1990. Marines were among the first U.S. troops sent to the Middle East. These troops were sent to help free Kuwait.

Many Marines are stationed on Navy ships throughout the world. They are part of an expeditionary force. When a war begins, an expeditionary force is sent to try and stop it.

Marines were stationed on the island of Diego Garcia in the Indian Ocean. More were stationed on the island of Guam in the Pacific Ocean. These Marines quickly sailed toward Kuwait. The ships carried tanks, trucks, planes, and weapons. U.S. military leaders also sent Marines stationed in the United States to the Middle East. All these Marines arrived within one week.

Marine Forces in the Gulf War

The U.S. military sent more than 90,000 Marines to the Persian Gulf. These members were both active duty and reserve members.

Soldiers faced many dangers in Iraq. Iraqi forces fired missiles at U.S. soldiers. U.S. soldiers had to watch out for land and sea mines. There also was the danger of Iraqi attacks with biological and chemical weapons. Biological weapons contain germs that spread deadly diseases. Chemical weapons contain deadly poisons. Marines had to wear special suits, masks, and boots to protect themselves against these weapons.

Iraqi troops also exploded oil wells in Kuwait. Fires from the oil wells created huge clouds of smoke. Many soldiers became sick from the smoke. The smoke also made it difficult to see enemy tanks and airplanes.

Soldiers wear special gear to protect themselves against biological and chemical weapons.

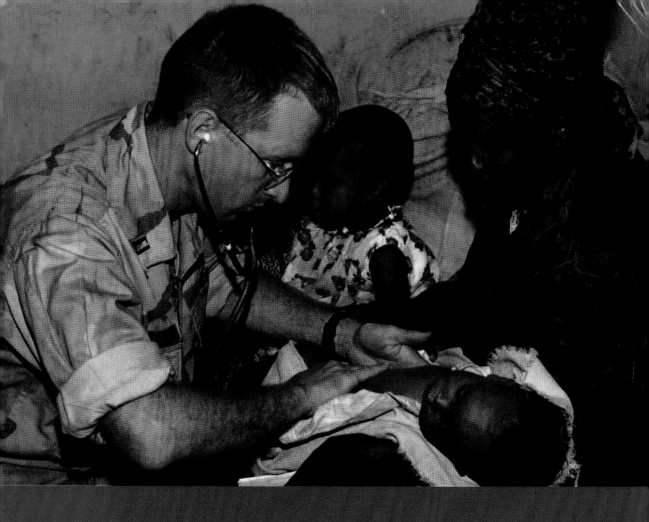

Marine doctors helped care for sick Somalians.

Weapons in the Gulf War

Marines used many types of weapons during the Gulf War. They fought with M-60 and M1A1 tanks. Infantry troops carried M-16A2 rifles and machine guns.

Marine artillery troops attacked enemy targets with howitzers. These large guns fire

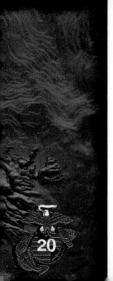

explosive shells. Artillery troops also launched missiles at enemy aircraft and ground targets.

Marines flew many types of aircraft during the Gulf War. They used F/A-18 Hornet and AV-8B Harrier attack jets to destroy enemy aircraft and ground targets. Marines used OV-10 Bronco and A6E Intruder attack planes to spy on enemy forces. Pilots used helicopters to carry troops and supplies where needed.

Marines in Somalia

During 1992 and 1993, Marines participated in Operations Restore Hope and Continue Hope. Several countries tried to help starving people in Somalia, Africa, during these missions.

Warlords stole the food that other countries sent to Somalia. The Somalian government was weak and could not stop these military leaders.

On December 9, 1992, U.S. military leaders sent Marines to Somalia. The Marines protected trucks bringing food to hungry people. Marine pilots used helicopters to deliver food to villagers where trucks could not reach.

Marine troops also helped repair roads, drill wells, and rebuild schools and hospitals. Marine doctors treated sick and injured Somalians.

F/A-18 Hornet

Function:	Fighter/attack aircraft
First Test Flight:	1978
Date Deployed:	1983
Length:	56 feet (17.1 meters)
Wingspan:	40.4 feet (12.3 meters)

The F/A-18 Hornet was originally built to be used by the Navy. But the F/A-18 Hornet also has become the Marine

Corps main fighter/attack aircraft. Pilots can attack enemy aircraft with Hornets. Hornets also can be used to fire missiles and drop bombs on enemy targets.

The Marine Corps began using Hornets during the Gulf War. They used them to destroy land targets and enemy aircraft. The Marines also used Hornets to perform reconnaissance missions. Pilots spied on enemy forces during these missions.

Currently, the U.S. military is working on improvements to the F/A-18 Hornet. New Hornets will be called Super Hornets.

CHAPTER 4

Learn about:

- **Special Forces**

- **Women in the Marines**

- **The LPD-17**

Marines are trained to quickly respond
to many emergencies.

Today's Marine Corps

The Marine Corps sometimes is called the military's "911 force." Marines are trained to quickly respond to emergencies. The Marines have helped during natural disasters such as earthquakes and forest fires. They have helped remove people from dangerous areas. They have helped provide people with food, water, and shelter during emergencies. Marines also have helped the U.S. government fight drug dealers.

U.S. military leaders believe that there is little chance of a major war in the near future. They believe it is important to train their troops for smaller conflicts. These conflicts are similar to the Gulf War and Operation Restore Hope.

New Training

The Marine Corps created the Marine Corps Sea Dragon Warfighting Laboratory. Marines use this laboratory to study new technology and fighting strategies. Marines take part in training exercises such as Hunter Warrior and Urban Warrior. These exercises teach Marines new ways to defend themselves against attacks.

The Chemical-Biological Incident Response force trains Marines to handle chemical and biological threats. This force has special equipment to detect chemical and biological poisons. The force also is trained to save people who are exposed to these poisons.

The Marine Corps Special Forces also will play an important part in future missions. The Marine Corps has two groups of Special Forces. The first is called Recon Marines. These troops perform reconnaissance missions. They spy on enemy forces.

The second is called Force Recon. Force Recon Marines perform reconnaissance missions. They also train to perform secret and dangerous missions. They may perform secret attacks on enemy targets. They may search for wounded U.S. soldiers in enemy areas.

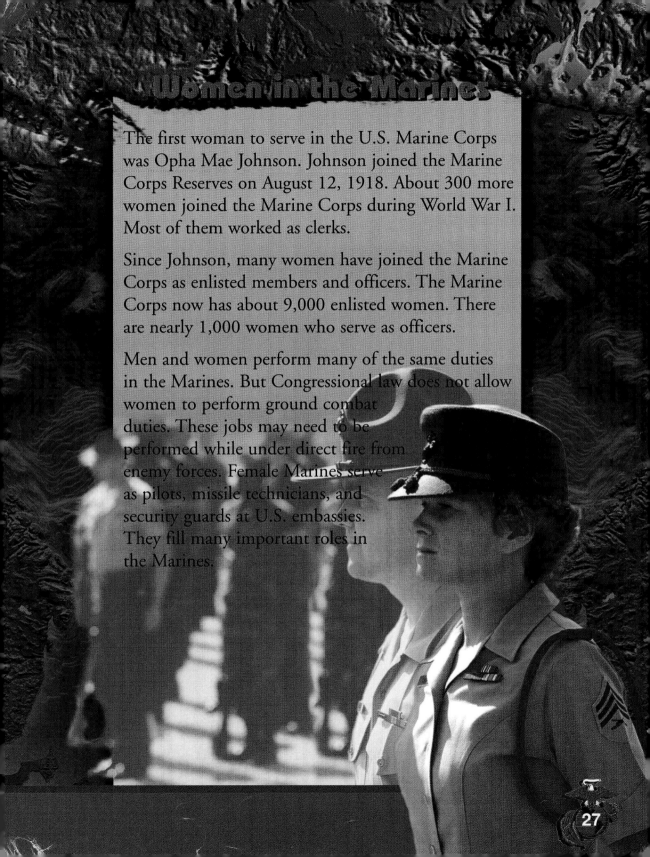

Women in the Marines

The first woman to serve in the U.S. Marine Corps was Opha Mae Johnson. Johnson joined the Marine Corps Reserves on August 12, 1918. About 300 more women joined the Marine Corps during World War I. Most of them worked as clerks.

Since Johnson, many women have joined the Marine Corps as enlisted members and officers. The Marine Corps now has about 9,000 enlisted women. There are nearly 1,000 women who serve as officers.

Men and women perform many of the same duties in the Marines. But Congressional law does not allow women to perform ground combat duties. These jobs may need to be performed while under direct fire from enemy forces. Female Marines serve as pilots, missile technicians, and security guards at U.S. embassies. They fill many important roles in the Marines.

New Equipment

The Marine Corps needs new equipment to accomplish modern missions. The Advanced Amphibious Assault Vehicle (AAAV) will allow faster amphibious landings. The AAAV can reach speeds up to 50 miles (80 kilometers) per hour on land and up to 45 miles (70 kilometers) per hour in water.

Marines use amphibious assault vehicles to travel on land and in the water.

The LPD-17 is a new amphibious ship. It will transport Marines and landing craft to shore. Helicopters can land on the LPD-17. The LPD-17 can transport more equipment than other amphibious ships.

The Marines plan to use more guided weapons in the future. These weapons include Advanced Laser-Guided Bombs. Marines point a beam of light at an enemy target. These bombs follow the beam of light to the target.

Future of the Marine Corps

In recent years, the U.S. government has cut the amount of money it gives to the military. The Marine Corps has been forced to close some bases because of these cuts. It also cannot afford to have as many members.

The Marines perform duties similar to other military branches. For this reason, some government officials want to disband the Marines. But the Marine Corps keeps proving its value to the military. Marines have performed their jobs successfully during recent missions. This ability continues to make them an important part of the U.S. military.

Words to Know

allies (AL-eyes)—people, groups, or countries that work together for a common cause

amphibious (am-FIB-ee-uhss)—able to work on land or in the water

artillery (ar-TIL-uh-ree)—large, powerful guns

disband (diss-BAND)—to remove a military unit from active service

enlisted member (en-LIST-id MEM-bur)—a member of the Marine Corps who is not an officer

grenade (gruh-NAYD)—a small explosive device that often is thrown at enemy targets

mine (MINE)—an explosive device; water mines float in the water; land mines are buried underground.

mission (MISH-uhn)—a military task

reconnaissance (ree-CAH-nuh-suhns)—exploring enemy areas to gain information

To Learn More

Green, Michael. *The United States Marine Corps.* Serving Your Country. Mankato, Minn.: Capstone High-Interest Books, 1998.

Rowan, N. R. *Women in the Marines: The Boot Camp Challenge.* Minneapolis: Lerner Publications, 1994.

Voeller, Edward. *U.S. Marine Corps Special Forces: Recon Marines.* Warfare and Weapons. Mankato, Minn.: Capstone High-Interest Books, 2000.

Useful Addresses

Marine Corps Division of Public Affairs
Headquarters Marine Corps
The Pentagon, Room SE-774
Washington, DC 20380-1775

Marine Corps Historical Center
Building 58
Washington Navy Yard
Washington, DC 20374-0580

Internet Sites

Force Recon Association
http://forcerecon.com

Marines Online
http://www.usmc.mil/marines.nsf/marinesmagazine

United States Marine Corps
http://www.usmc.mil

Index